PREACHING THE GOSPEL
OF THE
RESURRECTION

THE BEVAN MEMORIAL LECTURES

commemorating the life and work of the late Rev. Llewelyn David Bevan, B.A., LL.B., D.D., first Principle of Parkin College, Adelaide, are established and maintained by the Governors of the Parkin Trust, Incorporated.

These Lectures for 1952 were delivered at the Stow Memorial Church, Adelaide, Australia, on March 17, 18, and 19.

Preaching the Gospel of the Resurrection

D. T. NILES

Philadelphia
THE WESTMINSTER PRESS

FIRST PUBLISHED IN GREAT BRITAIN IN 1953
BY THE LUTTERWORTH PRESS

Library of Congress Catalog Card No.: 54–6325

To
My Father

WESLEY DURAIAPPAH NILES

Born: August 8, 1873
Died: May 24, 1942

His servants shall do him service; and they shall see his face; and his name shall be on their foreheads. Rev. 22:3, 4.

ACKNOWLEDGMENTS

To Doubleday and Company, Inc., New York, for the passages in Chapter 1 from *The Story of My Life,* by Helen Keller.

To the Australian Council for the World Council of Churches, for the passage in Chapter 1 from *The Stranger,* by Daya Arul Nithi.

To John Murray for the letter by Edward Wilson in Chapter 3, from *Edward Wilson of the Antarctic,* by George Seaver.

To the Student Christian Movement Press for the passage in Chapter 4 from *A South India Diary,* by Lesslie Newbigin, and for the extract in Chapter 4 from *The Cost of Discipleship,* by Dietrich Bonhoeffer.

All extracts taken from *The Bible: A New Translation,* by James Moffatt, are included by permission of Harper & Brothers, New York.

CONTENTS

For he must reign until he hath put all his enemies under his feet. The last enemy that shall be destroyed is death.
                                                            I Cor. 15:25, 26.

» 1 «

THE SIGNATURE OF HOPE

For Christ sent me . . . to preach the gospel: not in wisdom of words, lest the cross of Christ should be made void. . . . For seeing that in the wisdom of God the world through its wisdom knew not God, it was God's good pleasure through the foolishness of the preaching to save them that believe. I Cor. 1:17, 21.

THE SIGNATURE OF HOPE

A FATHER was on his knees. He was seeking to pray. In his hands was a telegram which read, "Your son David reported missing believed dead." (David was an air pilot.) Praying seemed impossible. He rose from his knees and went and sat at his table. He turned the telegram over, and almost unconsciously wrote on the back of it these words: "All that I have and all that I am I give to God and for his service." Once written, the words conveyed healing to his soul. He had answered the challenge of death. The telephone rang, and he received over it an offer of a place in a neighboring university. For Rev. Mathew Sands was a retired priest. He set out next morning to interview the head of the university and, taking an uncommon road, by chance came to a disused church bearing a placard: "For sale by auction." He entered, he knelt, and he prayed, and he decided to buy this church and make it again a house of praise.

Suddenly, there entered the church another man, Andrew Jelks, who too had come to see the property. He intended to buy it and make of it "Andy's Amusement Arcade." Sands and Jelks faced each other. Then Sands went home to calculate the amount he had in

the bank, as the total of all his savings, and to write a
letter offering this amount as his bid for the church.
Jelks was a far richer man, but Sands could do no more.
He looked at his letter, he looked at the words he had
written on the back of the War Office telegram, and then
he went out and posted his letter to the trustees.

When the day of the auction came, and all those who
had sent their offers to the trustees were gathered in
the church, Sands casually put his hand into his waist-
coat pocket and found there his letter. He had forgotten
to send the letter after all. It was too late now. The
trustees were filing in already. And then it happened;
for the chairman announced that the church was sold
to Mathew Sands. " His is the highest offer," the chairman said, " and none can be higher, for here is his bid:
' All that I have and all that I am I give to God and for
his service.' " Sands had sent his telegram by mistake
instead of the letter he had written. (This story appeared
in the *Reader's Digest* about three years ago and is here
quoted from memory.)

The call to preach receives its significance from the
nature of the response it demands. This response can
be no more and no less than " all that I have and all
that I am." It is not merely the highest bid a man can
make if he is to undertake the task of preacher; it is
also the only bid that is adequate to such a task.

But how does it happen that men are brought to this
act of self-offering? It happens by virtue of the fact that
the call to preach is a call to self-immolation. It shatters
the self, it brings the self to death, and it establishes the
self in obedience to a new task — that of proclamation.
A call to deeds would be more satisfying to the self;

but we, who have been called, are sent to preach. We
have been entrusted with the folly of preaching. Words
are our main responsibility.

Yes, it is true that we must testify to the message we
proclaim by lives lived under its compulsion, but the
message itself is not about any deeds of ours. All that
I have is God's, but I have nothing except his word
which found me and his word to the proclamation
of which I have been sent. All that I am is God's, but
I am not except that I am set as a signpost to point to
him and to his working in me in the world. Men hold
it as an axiom that their lives belong to themselves and
that human history is at man's discretion; but by the
very experience of our call to preach we know that this
is God's world, that man is God's creation, and that
human history is ultimately at God's disposal. We know
that not man's deeds but God's are decisive. We
know that God is a working God. "My Father is working still, and I am working," said Jesus (John 5:17).

The word of the Lord came to Jeremiah saying, "Jeremiah, what seest thou?" And he said, "I see the shoot
of a Wake Tree." And the Lord answered and said unto
Jeremiah, "Thou hast seen right. For I am awake over
my word to perform it" (Jer. 1:11, 12). This is the
charter of our preaching: that to us is committed God's
word and that God is awake over his word to perform
it. Our preaching is an activity within the activity of
God. It points to him. And it announces that his is the
deed by which man's peace is wrought. Indeed, our
announcement is that the deed is already wrought by
which man's peace is established and that, as we confront the problems and conflicts of our time, we are

bidden to share in the victory that God has already
won rather than seek to win victories of our own. " From
now on," said Jesus to Caiaphas, " you will see the Son
of man sitting at the right hand of Power, and coming
with the clouds of heaven" (Mark 14:62; cf. Luke
22:69). Here is the truth about human history — that
the Son of Man is sitting at the right hand of Power
and that he is coming with the clouds of heaven. Jesus
rules and Jesus comes — these are the loci of human
life. We cannot emphasize too strongly how foolish
such an announcement must seem to our contemporaries.

Can we then contract out of the preaching to which
we are committed? or preach differently? How can we?
Our standing ground is different from that of our contemporaries. They are seeking to make human history;
we know that we have been caught up into the divine
activity. One of the things that God has done in deal-
ing with his world is to get hold of us. That is why for
us the word has priority over the deed.

> " How beauteous are their feet
>   Who stand on Zion's hill,
>   Who bring salvation on their tongues,
>   And words of peace reveal! "
>
> (Isaac Watts).

The immediate word by which we are bound is the
word by which we were called, each one by name. We
can each bear testimony to the truth of that Scripture
which says: " I have called thee by thy name; thou art
mine " (Isa. 43:1). " Before I formed thee in the belly I
knew thee; and before thou camest forth out of the
womb I sanctified thee " (Jer. 1:5). We are members

of the "ecclesia"—the assembly of those who have been called by name. But this call, by which we are constituted, constitutes us messengers of that Word which is previous to the word which was our call. This previous Word is Jesus Christ. In Jesus God became man. But Jesus is more than an individual man. He is the head of the new humanity, the head of the body that is the Church. All men find their humanity in him. In him all men come together unto a perfect man (Eph. 4:13). In him is man's true life. In him God has loved the world, that whosoever believes does not perish but lives eternally. In him the sin of the world was taken away. In him creation came to a new beginning. He is the "firstborn among many brethren," the first fruits of them that are asleep. This previous Word of God, so structural to human history, is the deed to which God's call to each one of us points and from which it stems, so that our preaching must point back to it. Our deeds cannot take the place of our word because our word is greater than ourselves. It is a word about that Word by which we were constituted and on which we stand. As John expresses it, "The life was manifested, and we have seen it, and bear witness, and show unto you that eternal life" (I John 1:2).

It is impossible to overemphasize this connection between Him whom we proclaim, who is the word, and the word by which he has called us to proclaim him. Paul's affirmation is, "Christ sent me to preach the gospel." There is particularity in that first personal pronoun. It is not simply that Paul has undertaken a work that every Christian must do, but that to him has happened that which must happen to every Christian

individually and separately. Each must be found by
name, and sent. Dr. S. Jesudasan, of the Ashram at
Tirupattur, in India, used to speak of an ignorant shepherd lad in the village, driving his sheep to pasture,
whom he asked how many sheep he had. The lad said
that he did not know. How, then, he was asked, would
he at the end of the day be able to say whether all the
sheep were safely in the fold? " I know each sheep by
name," he replied, " and if any is lost, I know which
one it is." God's love is like that. It knows by name,
and to be sought and found by that love is to experience
a revolution of the soul. Let it happen to a person and
the needle of his life is set. Thenceforth it will always
point north.

But it is not enough simply to say that we are called
to preach. We must keep clear in our minds the truth
that our preaching never becomes independent of God's
call. His call is always present tense, so that there is
always living relation between what we preach and
what he does. Let me put it like this: I speak the word
of God as I have heard it and as I have understood it.
But if any of you who are listening to me should hear
God's word, it will not be because I have spoken God's
word, but because God has spoken it. I cannot speak
God's word. Only God can speak God's word. The
miracle, however, is that God in his grace takes human
words and makes them his word. Indeed, even as I
speak to you I am praying that God will take some
word of mine and make it his word for you. The
significant thing is not what I say but what God says
with what I say. The significant thing is not what we
do but what God does with what we do. Surely, it is

only because of this divine activity which supports our
preaching that we continue in this ministry of preaching
at all.

Preaching would be folly if it were not that preaching is simply the human contribution that is brought to
the service of the active operation of the word of God.
The easiest thing in the world is to talk, just as the
commonest thing in the world is bread. But here precisely lies the truth, that God takes the human word
even as he takes man's bread and makes them both the
means of his visitation. Through them he enters into
human life. " Lest man should glory" is Paul's explanation of this determination on the part of God that the
pre-eminence shall be his. How cheap words are! So
also is a kiss. A kiss is the cheapest thing that a lover
can give to his beloved. And yet it is just because it is
given, even though it is so cheap, that it becomes so
satisfyingly the mode by which personality is offered
and received. The insignificant has a quality all its own
in the relation between person and person.

Let me say again that I am neither disregarding nor
underestimating the importance and the necessity of
living lives that will commend our words, but that I
am seeking rather to emphasize the truth that the
determining fact is not that our lives prove our word
but that our word judges our lives. The truest testimony
that my life can bring to the word I proclaim is not
the life I live but what I think of the life I live. I
remember some time ago being at a meeting in India
at which someone asked Dr. Visser 't Hooft what
difference it would have made to the life of Mahatma
Gandhi if Mahatmaji had been a Christian. Dr. Visser

't Hooft's answer was something like this: " I do not think
he would have acted very differently with respect to
the main issues that he faced, but I am sure he would
have thought and felt differently about his actions."
The peculiar fragrance of the Christian life is not the
fragrance of one's actions, but the fragrance which is
the result of one's estimate of those actions.

In one of his lectures, Dr. John R. Mott said that
Prince Bernadotte of Sweden, in his last letter to him,
had made the remark that through a long life of
Christian living he had learned the meaning of saying,
" I am an unprofitable servant." When Jesus, in his
parable, made the publican say, " God be merciful to
me a sinner," he was expressing a judgment not so
much on human living as on human existence. There
is a world of difference between asking God to forgive
our sins and asking God to be merciful to us sinners.
The light of the Word must be so shed upon our lives
that men may be enabled to see our good works and
glorify the Father who is in heaven (Matt. 5:16).

Beyond the deed and over against it stands the word,
the word of which the deed is obedience, and the
word to which that obedience points. This insistence
on the word that must be preached may sound like
foolishness; but it is foolishness only to those who think
that by their wisdom they have either known God or
got rid of God. To us who have been waylaid by God's
call, preaching is power. It is the human offering
through which God's power is mediated to man.

Jesus was a preacher. He preached the nearness of
the Kingdom of God. But those who heard him found
it difficult to understand or accept his preaching. The

9066

things that he did seemed to them to point in different
directions. The Herodians were afraid of him because
to them he seemed to be too intense; the Zealots were
disappointed with him because to them he seemed to
be too obtuse. The Pharisees doubted him because to
them the Kingdom he announced seemed to be a
dangerous irrelevance, while the Sadducees hated him
because to them the pointed relevance of his announcement was only too clear. And then an incident happened.
He fed five thousand people with five loaves and two
fishes, with the result that it seemed to all who were
there that the crucial moment had arrived. The crowd
surged around him and offered him a crown. But he
would not accept it. He actually drove the crowd away,
including his disciples. They were all bewildered. They
could not see how there could be a kingdom when the
king refused to be crowned.

They waited for him on the other side of the lake
and, when he came, they decided to ask him one straight
and direct question which would settle all doubt. The
Pharisees and the Sadducees acted as spokesmen. They
came to him and said, "Give us a sign" (Matt.
12:38; 16:1). They were unbelieving and timid, but they
were willing to be convinced. The disciples too seem
to have been glad at this direct question. They too
wanted to know, and know once and for all, the truth
about the Messiah. (We remember how Jesus warned
his disciples after this incident to beware of the leaven
of the Pharisees and of the Sadducees.) But Jesus would
not give a sign. No sign, said Jesus, would be given
except the sign of Jonah. It is an adulterous people
that seek a sign, and they seek it because they are

already in adulterous relationship with other gods.

Nineveh must be saved, for God loves Nineveh. It is a "great city, wherein are more than sixscore thousand persons that cannot discern between their right hand and their left hand; and also much cattle" (Jonah 4:11). Therefore must the word of the Lord be proclaimed to Nineveh. The word to be proclaimed is the word of judgment. For it is God's mercy that he does not simply execute judgment but that, rather, he causes judgment to be proclaimed in order that men may repent. So it was in the preaching of Jesus, who came to Galilee in the power of the Spirit, saying, "The time is fulfilled and the kingdom of God is at hand; repent ye, and believe in the gospel" (Mark 1:14, 15). And Nineveh repented. It asked for no sign, it demanded no deed. The preaching of Jonah was enough. Jesus says to his questioners: "You too need no sign, nor will a sign be given. The word is proclaimed and that is enough. It is enough precisely because he who proclaims the word is Jonah. Jonah himself is the sign."

Jonah had tried to escape obeying God's call. He had no love for Nineveh, and he knew God's love for it. "I knew," he says, "that thou art a gracious God, and full of compassion, slow to anger, and plenteous in mercy and repentest thee of the evil" (Jonah 4:2). Therefore he hasted to flee from God's presence. Jonah did not want to be caught in the toils of the barrierless love of God. It was much simpler and more peaceful to stay with his own people. He also remembered how God's word had made a fool of Jeremiah, and how Jeremiah had suffered. It was better to let it alone. Besides, Nehemiah and Ezra had succeeded in building a world for Israel that was simple in its outline, and Jonah was happy to live in it. It was a world in which Israel was constituted the people of God and in which the rest of the world remained outside the interests of Israel.

But Jonah's confortable world was shattered. God's word had come to him. "The word of the Lord came unto Jonah the son of Amittai saying, Arise, go to Nineveh" (Jonah 1:1). But Jonah rose up to flee to Tarshish. With what result? He became a source of danger even to his fellows. He could go to sleep in order that he might not hear the disturbing voice of God, but they had to deal with the storm. They prayed to their gods, they made their ship lighter by jettisoning some of their cargo, they even tried to row to safety after discovering Jonah's disobedience, but to no purpose. A disobedient Church is a menace to itself and to the world until it casts itself again on God's mercy.

And Jonah said unto them, "Take me up, and cast me forth into the sea; so shall the sea be calm unto you: for I know that for my sake this great tempest is upon you." "Wherefore they cried unto the Lord, and said, We beseech thee, O Lord, we beseech thee, let us not perish for this man's life, and lay not upon us innocent blood: for thou, O Lord, hast done as it pleased thee. So they took up Jonah, and cast him forth into the sea: and the sea ceased from her raging" (Jonah 1:12, 14, 15).

So in one way or another God's judgment and mercy prevail, and the world becomes the means by which the Church is thrown upon the mercy of God. Nebuchadnezzar destroyed Jerusalem and left Israel at God's mercy in Babylon. The Soviet revolution destroyed privilege and has left the Church at God's mercy in Russia. . . . And thus it happens again and again. How much at God's mercy the Church is today in many countries of the world! And if, in some lands, the Church still finds security in the world, at least the future is menacing. An obedient Church is at God's mercy, for obedience springs from possessing no other security but God. A disobedient Church is also at God's mercy, for the world will not tolerate for long a disobedient Church.

But when Jonah fell into the hands of God, he repented, and because he repented he was delivered. How truly he witnesses to his experience when he says: "They that regard lying vanities forsake their own mercy. But I will sacrifice unto thee with the voice of thanksgiving. I will pay that which I have vowed. Salvation is of the Lord. I went down to the bottom of the mountains: the earth with her bars closed upon me for ever: yet hast thou brought up my life from the pit, O Lord, my God" (Jonah 2:8, 9, 6)! Jonah died, Jonah rose again. Henceforth his own death and resurrection will be the ground on which he will stand as he proclaims God's message, God's message which is death announced toward sin, and which is resurrection announced toward repentance and faith. God's love has made capture — it would neither let him go nor let Nineveh go.

We too preach because his love has found us, and because his love that found us is his love for others too. It compels.

> " O dearly, dearly has He loved,
>   And we must love Him, too,
>   And trust in His redeeming blood,
>   And try His works to do "
>   (Cecil Frances Alexander).

We must and therefore we try. But we can try only because we trust. His redeeming blood still redeems. Indeed, our preaching would be pure folly if it were
not that he whom we preach both upholds the activity of preaching and accomplishes the end toward
which the preaching is directed. Jesus who is proclaimed
is himself the power unto salvation. He is power to
uphold the preacher as well as power to prove the truth
of the preacher's message. God's power, which is power
over death in all its forms and in all its correlates
— sickness and suffering and sin, has been made manifest and operative in Jesus Christ. "He was declared
to be the Son of God with power, according to the
spirit of holiness, by the resurrection of the dead"
(Rom. 1:4). So that holiness and wholeness have now
become man's heritage into which he enters by himself
dying in Christ, being buried with him, and being raised
up by him unto life eternal. The preaching that is the
message preached — the kerygma — and preaching that is
the actual act of proclamation, both belong together in
one great divine activity. For God who raised up Jesus
from the dead has raised up us also and made us preachers
of the resurrection. We too have gone down into the pit
and have been delivered.

This definition of the relation between the preacher
and his message is the main argument of Paul in the
great resurrection chapters of his letters to the Corin-
thians and to the Romans. We are risen men speaking
about Christ's resurrection. We have shared in his death,
and now we share in his life. And if this was not true,
then neither was it true that Christ had been raised
from the dead. That is the point. Paul is not saying, " If

Christ is not raised up, then there is no resurrection of the dead"; what he is saying is, "If there is no resurrection of the dead, then neither has Christ been raised up" (I Cor. 15:13). Apart from our resurrection his resurrection is simply past tense, and preaching about a past event in the past tense is pure folly. The resurrection of Jesus Christ is power because it is past event as well as present operative reality. We have died with Christ, we have risen with Christ, and in Christ God has blessed us with every spiritual blessing in the heavenly places. We are those of whom the truth is to say, "As dying and behold we live" (II Cor. 6:9). It is true that we shall come to our death which will be the end of this earthly life, but that death will be no more than the physical counterpart of a death we have died already. And the resurrection that awaits us beyond physical death will be but the glorious consummation of the risen life which already we have in Christ.

"There shall no sign be given but the sign of Jonah the prophet. For as Jonah was three days and three nights in the belly of the whale: so shall the Son of man be three days and three nights in the heart of the earth. The men of Nineveh shall stand up in the judgment with this generation, and shall condemn it; for they repented at the preaching of Jonah; and behold a greater than Jonah is here" (Matt. 12:39–41). The preaching of the gospel of the resurrection by risen men — that is God's call to us and that is the call by which we are constituted preachers.

But how do we respond to this call? And what is involved in the experience by which it becomes determinative for us? Nothing less and nothing else is involved than the discovery of the nature of God's love. What is love's nature? Let me quote a passage from the life of Helen Keller which suggests the answer. She writes: "One day while I was playing with my new doll, Miss Sullivan put my big rag doll into my lap also, spelled d-o-l-l and tried to make me understand that d-o-l-l applied to both. Earlier in the day we had had a tussle over the words m-u-g and w-a-t-e-r. Miss Sullivan had tried to impress it upon me that m-u-g is mug and that w-a-t-e-r is water, but I persisted in confounding the two. In despair she had dropped the subject for the time, only to renew it at the first opportunity. I became impatient at her repeated attempts and, seizing the new doll, I dashed it upon the floor. I was keenly delighted when I felt the fragments of the broken doll at my feet. I had not loved the doll. In the still, dark world in which I lived there was no strong sentiment or tenderness. I felt my teacher sweep the fragments to one side of the hearth, and I had a sense of satisfaction that the cause of my discomfort was removed.

"She brought me my hat and we walked down the path to the well house. Someone was drawing water and my teacher placed my hand under the spout. As the cool stream gushed over one hand she spelled into the other the word 'water,' first slowly, then rapidly. I stood still, my whole attention fixed upon the motions of her fingers. Suddenly I felt a misty consciousness as of something forgotten — a thrill of returning thought; and somehow the mystery of language was revealed to me. Everything had a name. As we returned to the house every object which I touched seemed to quiver with life. On entering the door I remembered the doll I had broken. I felt my way to the hearth and picked up the pieces. I tried vainly to put them together. Then my eyes filled with tears; for I realized what I had done" (Helen Keller, *The Story of My Life,* pp. 22–24).

Everything has a name, and everything is an object of love — of God's love and therefore of ours. It is the nature of love to individualize. It is this conviction that must be wrought in the soul, and how is it wrought except by the soul's meeting with the Christ? Jonah met the living God and found himself caught in the toils of God's love. To God, Nineveh was not just a Gentile city — God knew it and loved it by name. And this love for Nineveh was part of God's love for Jonah. It is into this experience that we too must enter. We enter into it as we meet the Christ ourselves. For it is in that meeting that we are overwhelmed by his love which knows us and calls us by name, and also learn to love by name even as he does, so entering into his constraint to announce his love to all his beloved.

We must meet the risen Christ. But what does that mean? What do we mean when we speak of Jesus as one who is alive and whom we can and must meet? When the Jews crucified Jesus they were not worrying about the immortality of his soul. They did not care that Jesus would still go on living on the other side of death; all that they were concerned about was that Jesus should not live on earth any more. As long as he was on earth he wrecked their peace. They had to encounter him, and he confronted them, and they could not stand it any longer. So they killed him. But Jesus came back to earth. He rose again from the dead. He is on earth now. When we speak of the ascension of Jesus, we do not mean that he left this earth and went up to heaven. If that were so, the ascension would be a second death, a negation of the resurrection. It is no such negation. Jesus is both here and there, he is both risen and ascended. For him death is no boundary. We who are on earth are bounded by death, we are on this side of it; those who are dead are also bounded by death, they are on that side of it; but Jesus is risen and ascended, he is both on this side and on that. He has conquered death. How inevitable it is, then, that he should confront us, and that, when we awake to our encounter with him, we should be shattered by his presence and, being shattered, should also be stabilized by his love. " Jesus said to her, Mary. She turned and said to him, Rabboni. Jesus said to her, Go to my brethren " (John 20: 16, 17).

Our human frame is a natural protection against the awfulness of his holy presence; so also are the various disguises that we wear. We are cultured and know the disguise of courtesy. We have profited by the processes of character training and know the disguise of morality. We have most of us inherited a Christian tradition and know the disguise of religion. But somehow, sometime, somewhere, each one of us comes to his personal meeting with the risen Lord, and there stands stripped of every disguise, beseeching him to depart for whose abiding presence the soul longs.

Let me close with a meditation written by a woman in Ceylon about this experience. It comes from the heart of our Ceylon Church and says more simply than

I can say the truth of that about which I have been
speaking.

" Sir, come into my home.
 You look worn and tired.
 (But wait. Can I ask him to come into my humble, dirty
    home?)
 My home is humble, it is also dirty,
 but you are welcome to come in, if you do not mind.
 I always seek such homes,
 the Stranger replied as he walked in.
 Why, Sir! Your feet and hands are bleeding,
 and your hair is all matted with blood!
 Let me bring some water to wash it all away.
 No. Water cannot wash it.
 Then, what can?
 Love.
 Love!
 Yes, love.
 For whom is this blood shed?
 For one who has gone astray.
 I have followed her through the highways and byways of
    life,
 over rocks and mountains,
 and through valleys covered with thorns.
 Is she worth all this suffering, Sir?
 Yes, she is my child.
 Did you have to follow her long?
 Yes, for the last forty years.
 Did she never know that you were following her?
 She did.
 There were times when her path was far too difficult for her,
 and then she would stop and turn round and ask me to
    help her.
 I did, gladly;
 but when it was all over she would leave me and run away
    again,
 sometimes with never a word of thanks.
 She was swift of foot.

Did you keep on following, Sir?

Ah, yes, for how could I give her up? She is my child and
I love her.

She too must be tired and worn out. She too must be sore
and covered with wounds.

Yes, she is covered with them, both soul and body.

The soul which is meant to look beautiful and lovely, is
now ugly;

but still she is my child. How I long to heal her!

Does she not love you, Sir? That she must let you suffer
so?

I have glimpsed her love for me now and then,

but that which is before her eyes is something else and she
follows it blindly.

She never lets me come between her and the thing she
follows.

Is that thing which is before her so attractive?

Yes, to the natural eyes it is.

Who is this woman, Sir?

Who is she who made you suffer so?

There are blood drops all the way!

The Stranger looked at me,

and I too looked right into his eyes.

I knew him then.

I fell at his feet crying out,

My Lord and my God.

Arise my child, He said.

Let me, first, heal your festering sores with my blood which
I shed for you,

and let me cover you with my love.

I arose and looked at myself and saw how ugly I was

that I hid my face with my hands and cried,

Depart from me, O Lord, for I am a sinful woman.

But he put his hand upon me and would not let me go.

I felt his power go through me. I felt my burden roll away.

The whole of my past rolled up into one big scroll and
vanished from my sight,

and I heard Him say, It shall never return again "

                    (Daya Arul Nithi, *The Stranger*, pp 1–3).

So does God's love work, and so does Jesus make capture of men's lives. So also is there written over every Nineveh God's signature of hope.

" Blessed be the God and Father of our Lord Jesus Christ, who begat us again unto a living hope by the resurrection of Jesus Christ from the dead, unto an inheritance incorruptible and undefiled reserved in heaven for us, who by the power of God are guarded through faith unto a salvation ready to be revealed in the last time." Amen.

» 2 «

THE SIGNATURE OF DEATH

We hoped that it was he which should redeem Israel; but he is dead, and besides all this, it is now the third day since these things came to pass. Moreover certain women of our company amazed us. They came saying that they had also seen a vision of angels, which said that he was alive.

Luke 24:21–23.

» 2 «

THE SIGNATURE OF DEATH

B UT he is dead. Hope has come to an end. Sorrow is poignant. And there is nothing more to say. What does one say in the presence of death?

Some months ago I was attending a funeral service in Ceylon held on the occasion of the death of a respected member of the Church. The minister who was conducting the service preached a short sermon in which he spoke about death as a messenger of God and of blessing. While the minister was speaking there was going through my mind that verse of Scripture which says, "The last enemy to be destroyed is death" (I Cor. 15:26). When the service was over, and we were walking to the cemetery, I asked my friend what he thought of the saying of Scripture which spoke of death as an enemy, and how he reconciled that thought with the sermon which he had just preached. He shrugged his shoulders and said, "The important thing to do at funerals is to say something that will be comforting." Is it?

The comfort of sentimental talk is of small duration and of little value. The only true comfort is the comfort of truth. What is the truth about death? What does our Christian faith say about it? It says primarily three things:

First, that death is the consequence of sin.
Secondly, that death is God's provision for sinful man.
And thirdly, that death is already defeated.

Death is the consequence of sin. Human life is life lived outside the garden of innocence, and an angel with a flaming sword guards the entrance to it lest man should have access to the tree of life and live forever. We sin and grow old and die and see corruption. It is true that we are alive because God has forgiven us our sins, for if God dealt with us according to our sins, we should be dead and damned long ago. And yet, we who live by God's forgiveness, and even those of us who have learned to live in grateful response to that forgiveness, must die. By the symbol of the tree of life to which man has no access is the truth proclaimed that all existence, even forgiven existence, stands under the judgment of God on sin. Man must die. So that, when death comes, it comes as the last reminder we receive of the fact that we are sinners, men of unclean lips who dwell among a people of unclean lips.

But this death which is the consequence of sin is also God's provision for sinful man. It is good that sinful man does die. For life would be insupportable if men just grew old and older and never died. Now, at least, there is the possibility of quitting the stage of life with honor. Besides, it is because of death that man learns to live by faith in the faithfulness of God. All things undergo corruption; only God remains unchanged and unchanging, so that man who is girt about by death becomes aware of that grace of God which upholds him and over which alone death has no sway. Then, when at the last death comes, man makes his final act of faith, casting himself upon God's grace who, beyond death, will receive with forgiveness the human spirit.

> " Ready for all Thy perfect will,
>   My acts of faith and love repeat,
> Till death Thy endless mercies seal,
>   And make the sacrifice complete "
>   (Charles Wesley).

But death is also other than God's provision for sinful man. It is God's enemy. It constitutes the barrier between the life of earth and the life of heaven. God has constantly to cross this barrier to make himself available to man. In Jesus this barrier is permanently crossed. He entered through the gate of death and came back again. Death now is a breached wall, a defeated enemy. The life of heaven is now available, available to us on earth as a foretaste and as a first installment. In him by faith we " have been stamped with the seal of the long-promised holy Spirit which is the pledge and installment of our common heritage, that we may obtain our divine possession and so redound to the praise of his glory " (Eph. 1:13, 14).

Is it any wonder that Paul cries out:

> " O death, where is thy sting?
>   O grave, where is thy victory? "

For the sting of death is sin, and sin has been dealt with in Jesus Christ (I Cor. 15:55, 56). So that, for a Christian, simply to speak about death as a blessing and to call death a messenger of God is to be guilty of dangerous oversimplification. Death is an enemy to be faced victoriously, and if it is a blessing, it is only because in death grace encounters sin. When my father

died, a friend sent us a card on which she had drawn
a wall with a rose creeper creeping on it and disappear-
ing over the top of the wall. On the card was written
a verse which said, " The creeper on your garden wall
has flowered on the other side." It was beautiful but
it was false. Death is not a natural transition from this
life to the next. Death is an end, with all the startling
finality that belong to an end, while as for the beginning
that lies beyond the end, it is the result of death being
defeated by God's grace.

The Christian attitude to death is an attitude of
enmity. Death is something to be met and overcome.
And if a Christian is able to rejoice in meeting it, he
rejoices because Christ has enabled him to meet it
victoriously. It must also be said here that the sharpness
of death is most real, not when death comes to oneself,
but rather when death comes to those whom one loves.
But, even in such an experience, victory over death is
what the Christian faith offers. The sorrow that accom-
panies the bereavement of death is an inevitable sorrow,
but Christian sorrow is clean; it is not tainted either by
bitterness or by despair.

In one of the tribes of Africa, a family had been converted to Christianity. That was the beginning. Then
quite suddenly the only child in that family fell seriously
ill. The missionaries in charge of the work prayed as
they had never prayed before for the life of that child.
The whole future of evangelism in that place seemed
to hang on it. If only God in Jesus could be shown as
the conqueror of death, then all would be well. But to
their great dismay the child died. Some weeks passed.
And then one day there came to the missionaries' house

the leaders of the tribe, asking to become Christians. But why? the missionaries exclaimed. The answer was direct: " We want to worship the God who can teach men to die and to face death. We have never seen anybody die as that child died, or anyone face death as you and his parents faced it."

There has recently retired a missionary of the Church Missionary Society who was once in Ceylon — Rev. J. P. S. R. Gibson. When he was in Ceylon, his son, who came to visit him from England, was suddenly taken ill and died. Even today in Ceylon they speak of the funeral service that was conducted for Gibson's son, and of the short testimony that the father himself bore at the service to Jesus, proclaiming him as the resurrection and the life. The direct consequence of that service was the conversion of a Buddhist family to the Christian faith.

Ceylon is a land of many religions, and the heart of a religion is never laid more bare than in the way it meets death. When faced by death the Buddhist takes refuge in meditating on the nature of death's inevitability, while the Muslim bows in acceptance of death as the decision of Allah. Resignation is the keynote of both these religions in their attitude to death. The Hindu looks upon death as just one incident in a long series of births and deaths through which the soul must pass before attaining release. So that when death visits a home, those that mourn mourn without restraint. The person who is dead is ended as that person, and the conquest of death is complete. How important it is, then, that Christians should learn to witness to the gospel of the resurrection, and witness to it not least when they are visited by death.

How is the Christian victory over the experience of death won? It is won in that experience of true death which takes place when man meets God in the experience of conversion. " I have been crucified with Christ; yet I live. And that life which I now live in the flesh I live in faith, the faith which is in the Son of God, who loved me, and gave himself up for me " (Gal. 2:20). To have *metanoia* is to have the direction of one's will changed round. It is to sustain an inner collapse, to be disillusioned about oneself, and discarding one's trust in oneself, to entrust oneself to God and to his rule. After that, life becomes to live by faith, by commitment to Him who loved us and gave himself for us.

The source and secret of the Christian life lies in this transition that takes place when we come to rest in the love of God as it has come to meet us in Jesus Christ. We are moral persons under obligation to fulfill the law of love, and we strain and strive to fulfill it. Our lives become tense, and the moral imperative becomes terrifying. But the moment we see that the basic truth about ourselves is not that we are persons under the obligation to love, but that we are persons who have been loved, then the tension of our lives is eased and we become whole again.

The story is told of an incident that happened in Paris during those early days when surgery was still in its beginnings and anesthesia was not known. Two doctors were conversing together in a hospital about one of their patients who looked like just an ordinary peasant. They conversed in Latin, as they did in those days. One doctor said to the other, " The only thing to do is to operate"; to which the other replied: "Yes, and even if anything goes wrong there is no one to question us. He seems to be a man who has no relatives or friends." The patient, who was a monk, and who understood Latin perfectly, turned on his side and looked at the doctors and said, "Jesus died for me." John of the Cross in one of his meditations puts these words into the mouth of Jesus: Jesus says to him, "When I was hanging on the cross I thought of you and shed one drop of blood for you."

That is what I am. I am a sinner for whom Jesus died. I am just one of those who has been loved by God in Jesus at the cross. That is the central truth about me. All the rest is peripheral. I am a minister of the Methodist Church. I am an officer of the World Council of Churches. I have written and published some books. I am son and husband and father and friend — but none of these is I. I myself am simply he whose death God's love has encompassed, and who comes to his death in meeting God. When man meets God and is defeated by him, then has begun for him the victorious life. We must learn to live by this love with which we are loved. Only so do we learn to live at all. For we live most deeply when we live in the passive voice.

In my home I do not live as a person under obligation to love my wife and children. I live as a person who is loved by them. My wife does not live as a person under obligation to love me and the children. She lives as a person who is the object of our love. The children do not get up in the morning saying, "We must love Father and Mother." They simply live in the consciousness of the fact that they are loved. The commandments,

"Thou shalt love the Lord thy God with all thy heart, and with all thy soul, and with all thy strength and with all thy mind; and thy neighbor as thyself," are indeed commandments which we must obey. But they are commandments given to those who have been loved. The love of God and of man become a possibility only to those who know what it is to be loved. The desperate illness of our time is not that we do not love God and love each other, but that we do not know how to receive love either from God or from man. That we should be loved with all our smallness and our sinfulness, with all our self-conceit and our self-centeredness, that we should be loved even at the cost of death to Him who loved us, can anything else be more potent to break us down or build us up?

To be converted is to enter into the realization that God loves me and that he has loved me in Jesus Christ. Let this realization once flood the soul, and love will awaken love, until the imperative of the moral life becomes the consequence of the religious life. The self will then be lost in loving and being loved. We forget too easily that love has only one source and that is God, and that men cannot generate love in their own hearts. We can love only as God's love flows through us.

This death of self in the experience of conversion is the key to our victory over death. Paul could say, " For to me to live is Christ and to die is gain " (Phil. 1:21) — for when physical death came to him it could not touch him, since he was already dead and the Paul who lived in Christ was already living in Him who is death's conqueror. To die was not to die at all but to continue to live in Christ, gaining through physical death the enjoyment of the direct presence. This is the truth about the Christian life, that we are already in heaven, blessed with every spiritual blessing in the heavenly places in Christ, and that this situation conditions our attitude to the business of daily living. With respect to our work, our existence, and our relationships, we are as those who have died and continue to die daily.

The work we do, during our life on earth, is always work that somebody else has done. We begin where they have left off. And somebody else will begin where we leave off. "We inherit splendid towns which we never built, with houses full of stores which we never gathered, with reservoirs that we never dug, and with vines and olives that we never planted" (Deut. 6:10, 11). We inherit the results of the labors of those who have gone before us, and others who come after us will enter into what we have accomplished. There is a placard with the sign, "Move On," that hangs over all our work.

What is the consequence of this? The true consequence of this should be that in our working we should be delivered from bondage to results. We are too much concerned about results. We like to see the fruits of our labors. Some fruits we do see; but the long-range consequences of all that we do are in God's hands. We sow the seed and go to sleep; he controls the harvest, first the blade, then the ear, then the corn in the ear (Mark 4:28). He is the architect of history. How important it is then that we should never seek to blue-print our plans or adopt methods that are determined by our desire to see results! The desire to see results foreshortens vision and introduces into our planning a false perspective. It also introduces into our working a sense of strain. It is said of an old minister in a small church in Scotland, who was retiring at the close of a long ministry in that church, that there was in that church a layman who did not like this minister, and who, even at the last kirk session over which the minister presided, did not have the grace to keep quiet. He accused the minister of having achieved no results in his ministry. "How many have you converted?" he asked. The minister spoke humbly and said, "As far as I know, just one small boy." But neither the minister knew, nor his critic, that that boy would be a pioneer missionary in Africa for Jesus Christ. That boy was Moffatt, whose footsteps David Livingstone followed.

It is given to some of us to put one stone in place in the great city that God is building, but to many of us it is not given even to do this. All that we are allowed to do is to hew the stones in the quarry and to bring and offer them to God. But God is working, working all the time. Death has no dominion over him, and with him our work is safe. "Blessed are the dead which die in the Lord, for their works follow with them" (Rev. 14:13).

Our work must be dedicated to a future that is completely in God's hands, and, because it is so dedicated, we must find release from bondage to results, being enabled thereby to do our work with gladness.

But not only does the fact of death deliver the Christian in his work from bondage to results; it delivers him also in his life from bondage to existence. Life is meant to be invested, not protected. Existence, in itself, has neither meaning nor purpose. Nothing is gained by wrapping up one's life in cotton wool and preserving it across the years. To do so would be to accept defeat at the hands of death long before one dies. Death must teach us to live, and remove from us the desire simply to exist. Jesus was thirty-three when he died. "Not a golden hair was gray on his crucifixion day." "Our own hope was that he would be the redeemer of Israel, but he is dead." His death, however, is precisely the basis of our hope now. For when death came to him it did not come to him as his master; it came to him as his slave. "I lay down my life of my own accord," he said, "and I have power to take it again" (John 10:18).

There is in the book of Revelation an episode of two witnesses witnessing to God in the city which spiritually is called Sodom and Egypt, where also our Lord was crucified. And it was ordained that "if any man desired to hurt them, fire proceeded out of their mouth and devoured their enemies. But when they had finished their testimony, the beast that came up out of the abyss made war with them, and overcame them and killed them" (Rev. 11:5-8). As long as the work that was committed to them remained unfinished, and as long as they were engaged in the doing of it, they lived. No hurt could come to them; but when their work was over, they passed on.

It would be irreverent to argue that God's protection of his workers is an absolute protection, and that they can count upon being delivered from the normal consequences of their and other people's ignorance or mistakes or sins; but it is Christian faith to be concerned purely and primarily with doing the work that God has entrusted to us, and to trust him for the rest. Not a sparrow falls but he knows, and that is enough. I have

heard Dr. John R. Mott, one of the greatest Christian
workers and travelers of our time, refer to a card which
he said he always carried with him in his wallet. On it
was written, " With God, over the ocean; without God,
not over the threshold."

> " To Thee we rise, in Thee we rest,
> We stay at home, we go in quest,
> Still Thou art our abode "
>
> (Thomas H. Gill).

We are not competing in a race for longevity, nor
is existence the meaning of life. The meaning of life
is to live for God. God made man in his own image, and
man lives only as he reflects God, only as he lives in
responsive and responsible relation to him. A firm of
undertakers in Los Angeles sport this question on their
signboard: " Why walk about half dead when you can
be buried by us for 32 dollars? " Why indeed! " Let
the dead bury their dead," said Jesus; " you follow
me " (Matt. 8:22).

The fact of death delivers us in our work from bondage to results, it delivers us in our life from bondage to
existence, it also delivers us in our relationships from
bondage to ourselves. It teaches us to hold our loved
ones at God's disposal. It is the privilege of every
Christian to bear witness to the fact that, long before
death removed a loved one into the presence of God,
that loved one was already committed to God when
still on earth. Isaac is always God's.

In some parts of India there is the custom of making
vows to God when illness visits a home, and periodically
services are held in which these vows are paid. Rev.

Mr. Selvaratnam, one of my friends in Ceylon, has often spoken about an experience of his in conducting one of these services. The people stood in a queue and came up to him one by one while he stood by the Communion table. The first man came and said: "My goat was ill. I vowed eight annas. My goat is now well. Here are my eight annas." My friend had to receive the money, say a prayer for the man and his goat, and the man passed on. Then the next person, a woman, came and said: "My chicken was ill. I vowed two annas. My chicken got well. Here are my two annas." A prayer was said for her and her chicken, and she passed on. In the queue were a man and his wife. They came forward in their turn and said: "Our son was ill. We vowed one rupee. Here is our one rupee." My friend, missing the usual rhythm in what was said, looked at them and asked. "And did your son get well?" They answered, "No, he died." And then, seeing the look of puzzlement on my friend's face, they added, "Haven't we to pay our vows to God because our son died?" My friend said to me that he felt deeply humbled at that moment, because those simple people had a better understanding of the meaning of death and of the love of God than he did. In life as well as in death we are the Lord's, and those whom we love are the Lord's also. We have no right of possession over them.

There is growing up in the Church, in many parts of the world, a cult of the grave. The offering of flowers on Mother's Day at the graveside of mothers who are dead, holding services at cemeteries on Holy Saturday, lighting candles on tombstones on All Soul's Day, the laying of wreaths on death anniversaries —

all these practices, while they have something beautiful about them, yet constitute a real threat to the Christian witness against death. "He is not here, he is risen," the angel said to the women who came to the grave of Jesus; and by that resurrection are restored to us also in the communion of saints the loved ones for whose departing we grieve. We have not lost them in such a way that we have to go to the past to find community with them. They are with us always where, with angels and archangels and all the company of heaven, we laud and magnify his glorious name.

> " The grave is but a lie, 'tis life is truth:
>   And death, howe'er it comes, opens the door to God.
> To nurse the grievance of the grave is sin,
> And useless too to seek to understand
> The way in which the door of death swung open.
>   Your loved one has passed on:
> Regrets belie God's faithfulness and sap our faith,
> Memory hallows the things in time that are left behind,
> Then let attention seek eternal life:
> Friday is past, and Saturday too:
> It is Easter now "

(D. T. Niles, " Edna ").

"I believe in the holy Catholic Church; the communion of saints; the forgiveness of sins; the resurrection of the body; and the life everlasting." In the Church is our true relationship to each other, the relationship that undergirds all our human attachments, and which death can neither touch nor sever. "The gates of death never prevail against it" (Matt. 16:18). So that on earth or beyond the grave there is still true community, and community of life between all those who believe. For God is not the God of the dead but of the living (Mark

12:27). This conquest of death in the communion of saints is the result of God's forgiveness of sins. The sting of death is sin, the source of life is forgiveness. "He forgave us all our trespasses, we who were dead because of them, and he made us live with Christ, nailing to the cross that which stood against us, putting away from us the angelic rulers and powers" (Col. 2:13–15). This communion of saints which is a present reality is, however, only a foretaste of that which is to be. For when death itself shall be destroyed and also sin, we shall inherit together the risen body and the life everlasting.

Death is the boundary of our existence now. We who are on earth are on this side of death, while those who have died are on the other side. To them, as to us, death is a boundary. They are alive, but they are asleep. Neither theirs nor ours is yet the full waking life. But when death itself is no more, then it will be a new heaven as well as a new earth. It will be the risen life in its fullness and in its wholeness. "For as we have died with Christ so shall we also live with him, knowing that Christ being raised from the dead dieth no more. We shall grow into him by a resurrection like his" (Rom. 6:5–9).

"And I saw a new heaven and a new earth: for the first heaven and the first earth had passed away: and there was no parting any more. And I saw the holy city, new Jerusalem, descending from God out of heaven, all ready for her husband like a bride arrayed. And I heard a voice crying, Lo, God's dwelling place is with men" (Rev. 21:1–3). Death is, but death does not rule. It has no dominion over us. He who rules is the risen Lord. In him and unto him we live, bearing witness to the life eternal already become manifest among us, even though athwart all our human living there still lies the signature of death.

" Now the God of peace, who brought again from the dead the great shepherd of the sheep with the blood of the eternal covenant, even our Lord Jesus, make you perfect in every good thing to do his will, working in us that which is well pleasing in his sight, through Jesus Christ, to whom be the glory for ever and ever." Amen.

» 3 «

THE SIGNATURE OF LOVE

We know that we have passed out of death into life, because we love the brethren. He that loveth not abideth in death. Hereby know we love, because he laid down his life for us. And this is his commandment, that we should believe in the name of his Son Jesus Christ, and love one another.

I John 3:14, 16, 23.

» 3 «

THE SIGNATURE OF LOVE

Death is an event in time; it is also the nature of time. Time flows forward. It is and it is not. " As for man, his days are as grass; as a flower of the field so he flourisheth. For the wind passeth over it and it is gone: and the place thereof shall know it no more " (Ps. 103:15, 16). But it is by this quality of " flow " of transience and transitoriness, that time receives its depth. Man is not content just to drift on the surface of time. He must live. And to live means to conquer time's impermanence. How often we have said, speaking of our school days and our school friends, " Those days will never come back again "! And yet, by the very fact that we are able to speak of them, we show that those days, and the experience of those days, remain with us, not simply as memory, but as part of ourselves. We have, as it were, so lived those days that are gone that we penetrated the passing moment and plumbed its depth as it passed so that the experience of those days still abides.

Each moment is a dying moment. The signature of death is written across the face of time. But, because of this very signature, eternal value is given to every passing moment and man is challenged to taste eternity in time.

57

> " Fair daffodils, we weep to see
>   You haste away so soon:
> As yet the early-rising sun
> Has not attain'd his noon.
> Stay, stay,
> Until the hasting day
> Has run
>   But to the even-song;
> And, having pray'd together, we
>   Will go with you along "
>   (Robert Herrick, " To Daffodils ").

Time is met and transcended. But man's tragedy is that, because the present is fleeting, he tends to refuse to live in the present at all. He seeks to live either in the past or in the future. His life is beset either by nostalgia or by anxiety. To them who would live in the past Jesus says, " Everyone who drinks of this water will thirst again, but whoever drinks of the water that I shall give him will never thirst; the water that I shall give him will become in him a spring of water welling up to eternal life " (John 4:13, 14). While to them who would live in the future Jesus says: " Do not be anxious, saying, What shall we eat? or What shall we drink? or What shall we wear? Your heavenly Father knows that you need them all. But seek first his kingdom and his righteousness, and all these things shall be yours as well " (Matt. 6:31–33). The thirst of life is not quenched by water from the well of Jacob, however hallowed by past association that well may be: nor is life lived truly if anxiety about the future conditions its perspective. " Let the day's own trouble be sufficient for the day " (Matt. 6:34).

Whenever I seek to make clear to myself this quality

of time as possessing depth because of its very transitoriness, and whenever I seek to understand what it means
to live in the present and at depth, I find that the following two illustrations help me most. The first is an
illustration from the life of Sadhu Sundar Singh. He
went out one day to pray and spent his time of prayer
under a tree. When he finished praying and got up to go
he found that his whole body was swollen. He looked
at himself to discover that he had been stung by hornets.
He had disturbed a hive of hornets on the tree. They
had stung him while he was praying. But he had not
felt their sting during all that time that he was lost in
prayer (Streeter and Appasamy, *The Sadhu*, p. 134).
That was life in the present tense. The flow of time had
been transcended by life lived at depth. Jesus went into
the wilderness to pray after his baptism: he was so
lost in prayer that he forgot to eat, and when he finished
praying he found that he was hungry. This is the kind
of experience which tells us what life will be like
beyond the grave.

> " Father of Jesus, love's reward!
> What rapture will it be,
> Prostrate before thy throne to lie,
> And gaze and gaze on thee! "
>   (Frederick W. Faber).

My second illustration is the nature of our experience
when we are listening to a piece of music. The notes
that are heard at any one moment are heard along with
the total composition. The music that has already been
played and the direction of the whole movement are
part of every listening moment. There is a wholeness

of perception which is present throughout, so that the flow of music becomes a development and never a simple succession. Time is experienced in depth.

"This is eternal life, that they know thee the only true God, and Jesus Christ whom thou hast sent" (John 17:3). To know is to experience that personal inter-penetration which alone is true knowledge between persons. And to enter into this experience is to enter into a mode of life which transcends the nature of time as pure duration and simple succession. It is life in the present tense at depth, it is eternal life. So that when physical death comes to such as live this life it comes as sweet release. To die is gain indeed (Phil. 1:21). It is the final going home. We live as those who are dying, we die as those who are living. "He who believes in me," Jesus said, "though he die, yet shall he live, and whoever lives and believes in me shall never die" (John 11:25, 26). Lloyd Douglas, in his little book *Precious Jeopardy*, works out this theme of living in the present tense in the form of a very touching story. A home is going to pieces because the man of the home has simply succumbed to the tyranny of time, until through an accident he is led to expect death at any moment. Immediately, there is a change. He learns to live in the present tense, and harmony is restored to the home again.

"The day of death," says the writer of the book of Ecclesiastes, "is better than the day of one's birth" (Eccl. 7:1). It is better, not in the sense that it is better to die than to be born, but that, more than the day of one's birth, the day of one's death sheds light on the way of one's life. Animals die; it is only man who has to live, and hence only to man is it given to live with death as death's conqueror. The life of George VI is one of the freshest examples of the quality of life that is lived under the shadow of death.

But if the day of our death does shed light upon the way of our life, it is only because of the day of the death of Jesus Christ. He rose from the dead. And, in that he came back through the gates of death, we know that death is not an end but an exit, not a blank wall but an open door. Our Saviour Christ Jesus has abolished death and has brought life and immortality to light through the gospel (II Tim. 1:10). In the cemetery in Colombo there is a hall where the Buddhist dead are brought for the final rites before they are cremated. On the wall of the hall is the picture of a human skeleton. All life is transient, and death concludes life in meaninglessness, wherefore the Buddhist answer to the challenge of death is nonattachment. Death comes as the thief of life; therefore, the less we possess the less there is for death to rob us of. But on the wall of the hall at the cemetery where the Christian dead are brought, there is a cross. The human skeleton is the symbol of death's victory, the cross is the symbol of death's defeat. It is death turned into the means of life.

"Unless a grain of wheat falls into the earth and dies, it remains alone; but if it dies, it bears much fruit" (John 12:24). By nonattachment death can be cheated of much of the anguish it brings, but it can be overcome by love alone. Love increases the anguish of parting that is involved in death, but it robs death of its victory. To love is to die as the grain of wheat dies in order that it may bring forth fruit; it is to lay down

one's life for one's friends (John 15:13). Death is overcome when it is made the principle of life. A man loves
his country and because he loves he is willing to die
for it, even though under ordinary circumstances he is
a man who is frightened by measles, when measles has
come next door. A man loves his friends and because
he loves, even though death snatch them from his
physical presence, he is able to hold to them across
the gulf of death. The veil between them and him grows
thin, and he is there already beyond the veil with those
he loves. "Thus saith the Lord of hosts: If thou wilt
walk in my ways I will give thee a place of access
among these that stand by" (Zech. 3:7).

In his diary of the Antarctic Expedition, which Scott
and his friends undertook, Scott has made this record.
It is entered in his diary on the day that he and Wilson
went out together to their heroic death in the snow.
"We could have got through," Scott says, "if we had
neglected our sick" (George Seaver, *Edward Wilson
of the Antarctic*, pp. 290, 294). There is the victory of
love. It is in Wilson's last letter to his wife, however,
that we have the most perfect expression of love's
conquest of death which has come to us from that
epic struggle of those heroes who went out to conquer
the Pole. In it we have testimony not only to the nature
of death, as Christian faith faces it, but also to the
nature of that love which is always master of death
and of that hope which sees beyond the parting of death
to the meeting of eternal life. Here is Wilson's letter:

"To My Most Beloved Wife:
"God be with you in your trouble, dear, when I have gone.
I have written another short letter to you.

" I leave this life in absolute faith and happy belief that if God wishes you to wait long without me it will be to some good purpose. All is for the best to those that love God, and oh, my Ory, we have both loved Him with all our lives. All is well. . . .

" We have struggled to the end and we have nothing to regret. Our whole journey record is clean, and Scott's diary gives the account. . . . The Barrier has beaten us — though we got to the Pole.

" My beloved wife, these are small things, life itself is a small thing to me now, but my love for you is forever and a part of our love for God. . . . I do not cease to pray for you and to desire that you may be filled with the knowledge of His will. (*Later.*) God knows I am sorry to be the cause of sorrow to anyone in the world, but everyone must die — and at every death there must be some sorrow. . . . All things I had hoped to do with you after this Expedition are as nothing now, but there are greater things for us to do in the world to come. . . . My only regret is leaving you to struggle through your life alone, but I may be coming to you by a quicker way. I feel so happy now in having got time to write to you. One of my notes will surely reach you. . . . Dad's little compass and Mother's little comb and looking-glass are in my pocket. Your little testament and prayer book will be in my hand or in my breast pocket when the end comes. All is well." . . .

Wilson was a Christian. He believed. Let us, therefore, give also another illustration, this time from the life of someone who did not share the Christian faith, but who, by the very nature of love, was led to sense that victory which the Christian affirms over the experience of death.

Shelley knew little about the immortality of the soul, but he loved Keats so dearly that when Keats died, he awoke to the truth of the immortality of love. It is the immortality of love that is the basis of the immortality of the soul. We live because we are the objects of God's love. Let us listen to Shelley as the truth about immortality breaks through his song, because he loved so well.

> " That Light whose smile kindles the Universe,
>   That Beauty in which all things work and move,
>   That Benediction which the eclipsing Curse
>   Of birth can quench not, that sustaining Love
>   Which through the web of being blindly wove
>   By man and beast and earth and air and sea,
>   Burns bright or dim, as each are mirrors of
>   The fire for which all thirst; now beams on me,
>   Consuming the last clouds of cold mortality.
>
> " The breath whose might I have invoked in song
>   Descends on me; my spirit's bark is driven,
>   Far from the shore, far from the trembling throng
>   Whose sails were never to the tempest given;
>   The massy earth and spheréd skies are riven!
>   I am borne darkly, fearfully, afar;
>   Whilst burning through the inmost veil of Heaven,
>   The soul of Adonais, like a star,
>   Beacons from the abode where the Eternal are "
>   (P. B. Shelley, " Adonais," liv, lv).

The correlate of death is not birth except in the case of the race. The true correlate of death is immortal love. It is only in the case of the race that birth has to make good the ravages of death, and death is conquered by the living on behalf of the dying. This fact is finely represented in the central column of statuary that stands in the garden of statues in Oslo, in Norway. In this column is shown the progression of life, the progression being represented by human figures — men, women, and children — standing on each other and reaching upward. But the column is broken at the top, for progression is not by itself progress toward a goal.

In the Old Testament death is understood primarily as an event in the story of the race. Hence it is that in the Old Testament the immortal destiny of the people of Israel is what holds the center of attention, while the continuance of persons as persons beyond death is left undefined in a world of shadows. The Greeks did think of death as an event in the life of persons, but they were shut into seeking victory over death in the nature of human personality itself. (It is to Plato that we owe the belief that man is an immortal soul in a mortal body.) Hence the failure of the Greeks to overcome death in their thinking and believing, except that they overcame it by their perception of the very magnificence of the tragedy of death. There is something heroic in the sadness of Greece in the presence of death. It is in the New Testament that death is seen to be an event in the life of a community of persons. It happens to persons, it also happens in the community, for elementally the life of the Christian who dies is the life of the Church of which he is a member, which life is already life beyond death. Love is the relationship by which we exist within this fellowship. "We know that we have passed out of death into life, because we love the brethren" (I John 3:14).

We are persons because we have been made in the image of God. Trees and birds, mountains and stars are what they are by themselves. Man alone has been created a dependent creature. He alone is dependent on his relationship to God for his very humanity. Man

is man only as he mirrors God. The image relationship
conditions his existence. The dogness of the dog is in
the dog, but the manness of the man is not in the man.
It is true that we mirror God only fragmentarily because
we are broken mirrors. Sin has shattered our wholeness.
But still we mirror him, and will continue to mirror
him however fragmentarily, as long as he does not leave
us alone. It is he who maintains the relationship
between him and us. Man can deny the relationship
if he likes, but he cannot destroy it. Man cannot get
rid of God. And because he cannot get rid of God he
is immortal. God loves and God's love never dies. Man
is not an immortal soul in a mortal body. Man is body
and soul — a total person — in an immortal relationship
to God. Man is made in God's image. This relationship
is immortal. God does not allow his holy ones to see
corruption (Ps. 16:10).

Let us then look again at the nature of the Christian
life and its quality as a foretaste of the life that is to
come, a kind of dress rehearsal of the drama that is to
be. The characteristics of that future life are life in the
eternal present, life at God's disposal and life in the fellowship. These constitute also the true characteristics
of Christian life now. We must learn to live in the
present tense. We must rejoice to remain at God's disposal. And our relationship to each other must be such
that death, instead of breaking the relationship, is
broken by it. It is impossible to exaggerate the consequence for our life here on earth of this understanding
of it as the life of heaven under earthly conditions, nor
should we forget that sacrament of the Church in which
is centered the meaning of this mystery. In this sacra-

ment is divine food for earthly sustenance, there God
is offered to man and man to God, and there is realized
the worship of heaven in the worship of earth.

> " Feast after feast thus comes, and passes by;
>   Yet, passing, points to the glad feast above,
>   Giving sweet foretaste of the festal joy,
>   The Lamb's great bridal feast of bliss and love "
>   (Horatius Bonar).

We have spoken so far of the nature of death and
of life. We come now to the question at which we
always arrive when we speak about death: the question,
Where are the dead? They are God's now, they are in
God's hands, they are in God's presence. "Beloved,
we are God's children now; it does not yet appear what
we shall be, but we know that when he appears we
shall be like him, for we shall see him as he is"
(I John 3:2).

The nature of personality must be the clue to our
understanding of the nature of life after death. When
a child is born into the world, it is born an individual,
but by the very fact that it comes attached to its mother
it possesses the seed of personality. This growth in
personality begins straightaway. Personal relationship
is established between the child and its mother, the
child and its nurse, the child and its father, and so on.
As the child grows it becomes more and more of a
person and less and less of an individual. Personality
consists in the range, variety, and depth of our relationships. It is the operation of the "image" relation which
is the basic factor in human personality. In heaven we
shall be fully persons and cease completely to be

individuals. We shall retain our differentiation as persons, without that differentiation being expressed in the exclusiveness of individuality. We shall retain personal identity within a complete harmony. The relationships of earth will be fulfilled in heaven, except that the implications of exclusiveness in those relationships will have ceased to have meaning. An illuminating example is in the teaching of Jesus with respect to the most exclusive of human relationships — "When they shall rise from the dead, they neither marry nor are given in marriage, but are as the angels which are in heaven" (Matt. 22:30). There is only one marriage relationship there, that of the Lamb to his bride.

There is also another aspect of the life after death which Jesus emphasized, a belief to which we must cling in all our thinking. "Let not your hearts be troubled," he said, "trust in God: trust in me also. In my Father's house are many resting places. Were it otherwise, would I have told you that I am going to make ready a place for you? And if I go and make ready a place for you, I will return and take you to be with me. I shall come and take you, I am the way" (John 14:1–3, 6). So to us who seek to live by faith on earth is made available the life of faith beyond the grave. We put our hands into his hands and he takes us across, from resting place to resting place, each place already prepared with his presence, until at last we are led into the very presence of the Father. Our life on earth is a period of pilgrimage, it is our journey from Egypt to Canaan; our life beyond death is a period of settlement, of our inheritance of the land of the saints. Our earthly life is not an examination to be passed; it is a journey to be begun. What we must decide is the direction in which we will journey.

But is there not also another place that God has prepared, another type of existence called hell? No, a thousand times no. Hell is not God's preparation — it is man's nightmare. It is what happens to man when he steps out beyond death secure in his own competence, seeking to live the self-centered life in the company of the saints. To be in hell is to be shut into our own devices, and yet not to be left alone but to be troubled by the presence of God. I have already referred to my friend, Rev. Mr. Selvaratnam. Let me use another story of his as an illustration of what I am talking about. He was working in his room one morning when a young lad came to see him. He asked him what he wanted, and the lad said, " I just came to see you." So they sat together for some minutes, the lad refusing to speak and Selvaratnam waiting for what the lad had come to say. Then suddenly the lad broke down weeping and stammered out, " I have taken my life away from the hands of God, and I don't know what to do with it." That is hell.

There is hell because man is free to choose to be in hell; because man is free to refuse to love or to forgive or to be forgiven. But hell is hell because God refuses to stop loving even those who would be in hell. There is a hymn of Charles Wesley, the unexpected climax of which is this thought about hell:

> " Jesus, my all in all thou art;
>   My rest in toil, my ease in pain;
> The medicine of my broken heart;
>   In war my peace; in loss my gain;

My smile beneath the tyrant's frown;
In shame my glory and my crown:

" In want my plentiful supply;
    In weakness my almighty power;
In bonds my perfect liberty;
    My light in Satan's darkest hour;
In grief my joy unspeakable;
    My life in death, my heaven in hell "

(Charles Wesley).

Heaven in hell! How inexplicably triumphant! We are
not required to achieve logical consistency in what we
say about hell. Hell is not a place about which we can
speak objectively. We can speak of it only as a predicament in which men can choose to be. So that all that
we are required to say is that hell is a real possibility,
and that the choice of hell, when it is made, is always
made without a time limit. Existence in hell, when there
is such existence, has always the quality of eternity.
But, and this is where the crux of all speaking about hell
lies, no man has a right to speak about hell who does
not feel a real concern about those who shut themselves
up to that way of life. History opens with the question,
" Cain, where is Abel? " History cannot close until the
answer has been given to the question, " Abel, where is
Cain? "

In the minds of many people hell has no other
significance except something to be afraid of. It is not
possible to go to heaven by living a life that is directed
by the fear of going to hell. Such fear will eliminate
moral significance from all action. The only significance
of hell in Christian thinking is that it is a cause of real
concern. " If my mother should go to hell," said Sadhu

Sundar Singh, " I shall ask God to send me there." Surely the Sadhu was right in saying so, for he could go to hell with God. God was there already. God's love is a love that never lets go. " I will go after that which is lost, until I find it " (Luke 15:4).

> " As long as there is one man in prison, I am not free.
> As long as there is one man ill, I am not whole.
> As long as there is one man lost, I am not saved."

There can be no aristocracy of salvation, nor can the rule of Christ be anything but the rule of the Crucified. Too unconcernedly we speak about those who are not saved. The famous Spurgeon is said to have been so depressed by the attitude of the saved, that he prayed, " O God, save the elect, and elect some more." Heaven is not the Kingdom of the good, it is the Kingdom of love.

What, then, about the judgment of God? Jesus made it plain that God's judgment is always of persons and not simply of their actions. In a court of law, it is some deed which is being judged, some deed of which a person is held guilty or not guilty. But God judges the person himself. There were those who prophesied in God's name and in his name cast out devils. Their actions were good, but they themselves were declared to be unknown to God (Matt. 7:23). There were those who had fed the hungry and clothed the naked and entertained strangers and visited the prisoners, and they were declared to be inheritors of the Kingdom; but, and the story turns on that fact, they did not know that they had done all these things to Jesus (Matt. 25:37–40). What they had done was a true expression of themselves; it was unconscious fruit-bearing. Not their deeds, but that their deeds flowed from their true selves, was what was of significance. It was they who were judged.

And precisely because God judges persons and not actions his judgment can never be understood as retributive in intention. In his judgment of persons God is simply concerned with the best way of loving them. Love alone is justice to persons. God is stern and uncompromising because he is Love. With respect to those whom we truly love we too never let down our standards. We are indulgent only with respect to those for whom we do not care. God loves and, because he loves, he is terrible. His loving eye sees every blemish, and his hand does not rest until that blemish is removed. In his sculpture piece called *Hand of God,* Rodin expresses this truth in an arresting way. God's hand is seen holding the human form, and while the fingers are supple, molding the clay, the thumb is inexorable and relentless. "For Jesus must reign until" — until the purpose of that reign is accomplished; since the reign itself is a necessity born of God's purpose to redeem.

In this reign the saints too participate. This is the final truth we must look at about the nature of life after death. By his blood he has ransomed men for God, and has made them a Kingdom and priests to God, and they shall reign on earth (Rev. 5:9, 10). The saints are a royal priesthood (I Peter 2:9) called to share in the reign of the Crucified, to die with him and so to live with him, to endure and so to reign with him (II Tim. 2:11). The saints complete what remains of Christ's afflictions for the sake of his body, the Church (Col.

1:24). Death makes no difference to this occupation of the redeemed. They serve the reign of the Crucified here, they also serve the reign of the Crucified there. Their service is in his temple (Rev. 7:15), where the sacrifice of love is offered and the purpose of redemption is pressed.

When I was studying at Bangalore, at the Theological College, Bishop Badley of the Methodist Episcopal Church of North India came and visited us there. In a sermon he preached during that visit he hold us this story: He said that a son of his who was preparing to come as a missionary to India had suddenly been taken ill and died soon after completing his university course. "I was heartbroken and perplexed," he said, "for it seemed to me that the promise of my son's life was destroyed, and it was a life dedicated to God's service. But one night, a few days after my son's death, I dreamed that God spoke to me and said, 'I am using your son on this side.'" The ministry of redeeming love which is the work of the Christian is a ministry undisturbed by death, for Jesus must reign until he has put all his enemies under his feet, and his saints reign with him.

We often make anxious inquiry as to whether some loved one who has died died because it was God's will that he should die. There is no reply to such inquiry. God cannot will death; he can only will life. But God, who willed that his Son should accept death when it came to him, can will that we too accept death — death comes to us in different ways and for different reasons — and then, when death has happened, take us to himself, and for himself.

Thus is death challenged at every step by love: the love of God being set over against the hell within which men continue to shut themselves; men's share in God's work of love being set over against the intervention of death in their earthly lives; the communion of saints being set over against the parting that death brings between those who love; man's love for God being set over against the creatureliness of his existence.

Across the face of life is written the signature of death. But it is a signature that has been crossed out. And on the cross we see another signature, God's signature of love.

"Now may our Lord Jesus Christ himself, and God our Father, who loved us and gave us eternal comfort and good hope through grace, comfort your hearts and establish them in every good work and word." Amen.

» 4 «

THE SIGNATURE OF LIFE

Lord, thou hast been our dwelling place in all generations,
Before the mountains were brought forth,
Even from everlasting to everlasting, thou art God.
Thou turnest man to destruction, and sayest, Return, ye chil-
dren of men.
For a thousand years in thy sight are but as yesterday when
it is past,
And as a watch in the night.
In the morning they are like grass which groweth up;
In the evening it is cut down, and withereth.
For we are consumed in thine anger; thou hast set our in-
iquities before thee,
Our secret sins in the light of thy countenance.
All our days are passed away in thy wrath; we bring our
years to an end, as a sigh.
Return, O Lord; how long?
O satisfy us in the morning with thy mercy,
That we may rejoice and be glad all our days.
Let thy work appear unto thy servants, and thy glory upon
their children.
Let the beauty of the Lord our God be upon us,
And establish thou the work of our hands.

Psalm 90.

» 4 «

THE SIGNATURE OF LIFE

I N THIS great hymn of life and death there are worked
out the two themes that belong together: man's dying
because he is a sinner, and his living because he is
loved by God. It is only as we understand these two
themes as interpenetrating one another that we understand at all the nature of man's life. He lives as one
who is about to die. And yet he who is about to die is
the object of God's saving work. There is salvation in
the presence of death.

In The Acts of the Apostles is an incident that
illustrates this truth with great force, and that takes the
meaning of this truth even farther. It is the incident of
Paul and Silas and the Philippian jailer. Paul and Silas
were prisoners for the word of God. They had been
beaten, and, the magistrates having delivered them to
the jailer, they had been made secure in the inner
prison. The jailer, his work done, was asleep. Suddenly
he awoke with a start. He found the doors of the prison
open. He did not know what had happened except that
he himself was now in mortal danger. Surely the
prisoners had escaped. What explanation could he give
to the magistrates in the morning? He would certainly
lose his job, he would probably lose his life. It was
better to die by one's own hand than to die in disgrace.

77

He drew his sword to slay himself. A voice came ringing out of the darkness: " Do thyself no harm: for we are all here." It was the voice of the man from the inner prison. The jailer called for lights and, going running to Paul and Silas, cried out, " Sirs, what must I do to be safe? " The answer of Paul and Silas lifted his question out of its context. They said to him: " We cannot tell you what you must do in order that you may be safe when the magistrates come demanding an explanation. You might still lose your job or even lose your life. But we know how you can be safe whatever happens, and not only you but also your wife and children. ' Believe in the Lord Jesus, and you shall be safe, you and your family '" (Acts 16:19, 31).

The word of God is thrust into some inner prison and its insistence made fast in chains. The doors are locked, and life seems smooth and secure. Suddenly there is an earthquake, and there yawns before life the awful imminence of death. How can safety be found again? It can be found only in Him with whom we are always safe whatever may overtake us. " I have become absolutely convinced that neither Death nor Life, neither messenger of heaven nor monarch of earth, neither what happens to-day nor what may happen to-morrow, neither a power from on high nor a power from below, nor anything else in God's whole world has any power to separate us from the love of God in Jesus Christ our Lord " (Rom. 8:38, 39).

Two men went to build houses for themselves. One man bought a piece of land on a dried river bed. The land was cheap and building on it was easy. There had been no water in that river for years and years.

The other man built his house on high ground. It was hard to sink the foundations but he did it. Then the rain descended; it descended on both houses. The floods came; they swirled around both houses. The winds blew and smote; they smote both houses. But only one house fell. The other was safe (Matt. 7:24–27; Luke 6:47–49). Safety is safety in the storm and not from it; it is safety whatever happens. There is no shelter from the circumstances of life that is promised to the Christian, though God in his kindness does often give us shelter. He knows that we are children. But that which is promised is safety. He has promised to abide with us if we will build on him.

Henry Francis Lyte was a dying man when he wrote his great hymn " Abide with Me." He was leaving his native England for Italy in the forlorn hope of recuperating his health, and the hymn was written on the eve of his departure. No other hymn in the English language witnesses more convincingly to the serenity of a life that is safe with God. But what is sometimes not recognized is the paean of victory that sounds in that hymn. The present tune to which we sing it is a tune of quiet commitment. It is an evening tune with a downward slant. But the tune which Lyte himself composed for it was a tune of a different kind. In it the last phrase — " abide with me " — which comes at the end of every stanza is a phrase that begins with a note of ascent.

" I fear no foe, with Thee at hand to bless:
  Ills have no weight, and tears no bitterness.
  Where is death's sting? Where, grave, thy victory?
  I triumph still, if Thou abide with me.

" Hold Thou Thy cross before my closing eyes;
  Shine through the gloom, and point me to the skies:
  Heaven's morning breaks, and earth's vain shadows flee:
In life, in death, O Lord, abide with me "
                                   (Henry Francis Lyte).

But the inwardness of this experience of safety is not fully understood if it is understood simply as teaching us that Jesus Christ is the ground of our safety in our every extremity. We tend to speak of God only in terms of man's extremity. We find that man's life is bounded by death, that at the frontier of his life there is always the experience of guilt and of sin, and we speak of God's relevance to this situation of man. But what we learn from the story of the Philippian jailer is that the insecurity which belongs to human life is not present merely on the edge of life but at its very center. With every new gain in human knowledge, whereby man has been enabled to look after himself, the role of God in man's life has been pushed farther and farther out until now God comes in only to answer the question of guilt and sin and death. What we need to realize is that these questions are not properly asked unless they are asked as questions about the very center of human existence. Man does not become unsafe, he is always unsafe, and always there is present the question: What must I do to be safe?

" The nations raged, the kingdoms were moved; he uttered his voice, the earth melted. Come, behold the works of the Lord, what desolations he hath made in the earth " (Ps. 46:6, 8). Here is true description of man's real danger, for man's insecurity arises from God himself. Again and again in human history there arrive the apocalyptic days of the Son of Man, when his angels set their sickles to the harvest and when death hangs over all life and all of life. But this experience, which is periodic in human history, is an ever-present possibility in the lives of men as individuals. Each man stands in imminent danger of falling into the hands of the living God, and, when that danger happens, who will keep him safe? " Believe on the Lord Jesus Christ and you will be safe." Only Jesus can keep us safe when we come to our decisive meeting with God. Man in Jesus meets God in Jesus, and that is safe meeting. He is our advocate with the Father, the propitiation for our sins (I John 2:1, 2). In him the Father's love has reached us as holy demand, and by him we are enabled to respond to this demand in dedicated living. The creature is given authority to become a son, for, to as many as received him, to them gave he the right to become children of God, even to them that believe on his name (John 1:12).

There is also an obverse of this truth which must be remembered, and that is that not only does Jesus keep us safe in God's presence but he also keeps God safe for us. Life is difficult and riddled with problems, and there is always the possibility that the clouds of life will hide for us the face of the Father. Men lose God in the turbulence of life. Their grip on him grows weary and they let go. But for him who has met God in Jesus, God is always safe. Jesus keeps him safe for us. A little child addressed her prayer to God, and she ended her prayer with these words: " And, darling God, look after yourself, because if you are lost we are sunk."

Listen to this story from one of the mass movement

areas in India (Lesslie Newbigin, *A South India Diary*, pp. 89, 90):

" Some leather workers have been converted. They belong to the lowest social stratum of the villages, and their conversion has been bitterly resented by the Hindu landowners. The Christians have been denied access to, wells, and have been refused their customary employment. They have been crushed lower and lower by hunger and despair. At one moment there was a very serious weakening. Fourteen of the Christian men, driven to dull despair by hunger and unemployment, decided to submit. ' What is the good of it? What's the good of all this misery for the sake of a little bit of ash? Come on, we'll go and put it on.' [The converts had refused to smear their foreheads with the sacred ash of Siva when they were sent out to do the drumming for a festival.] They went in a body to the Hindu temple, telling the priest of their intention. Two crowds were watching. On one side, between the temple and the outcaste quarters, the Christians who had learned of the defection stood at a distance and watched. On the other side stood the Hindus. The fourteen men stood in a line in front of the temple. The priest went into the dark inner chamber of the temple and came out with the sacred ash to be given to each man. But something had happened in those men's minds. Instead of holding out their hands to receive it, they simply stood with arms folded. In the stupor of hunger and despair they had agreed to do this thing, but when it came to the moment, they could not deny their Christ. There was a moment of silence, when they stood on the very brink of apostasy. Then one after another spoke: ' Do what you will; we cannot do this.' Together they turned and walked back toward their fellow Christians. In a moment they were joined by their brethren, and the whole company marched back to the squalid slum that was Christ's outpost in that village, and the priest of Kali stood alone before the temple with the sacred ash still in his hand."

Those men in their distress had lost their grip on God, but God was not lost. Jesus kept God safe for them. They had met God in Jesus; now Jesus kept them and God safe for one another.

"I know him whom I have believed and he is able to guard that which I have committed unto him against that day" (II Tim. 1:12). What is it that I have committed to him? I have committed to him my very belief in God. When God met me in Jesus, I said, "Yes," and that "Yes" is safe with Jesus forevermore.

"Believe"—that then is the key word. Believe, and you will be safe. But what is it to believe? It is that by which we find ourselves participating in God's activity. "The time is fulfilled, and the kingdom of God is at hand: repent ye, and believe ye in the gospel" (Mark 1:15). This was the announcement of Jesus as he began his ministry. The hour has struck, God's Kingdom has arrived. You have only to stretch out your hand and you can touch it. God, who from the beginning of creation has been waging relentless war against the powers of darkness, has now launched his main attack. The strategic battle has begun. He has come as a thief comes, to bind the strong man of the house and to despoil it (Mark 3:27). How apt Paul's description of evil is when he speaks of it as "dethroned" (I Cor. 2:6). The strategic battle was won by Jesus, and evil has been cast down, though it is still alive and active and will be so until God's V day comes.

In Mark's Gospel, the enemy against whom God has declared was in Jesus is described in terms of five miracles which follow one another in quick succession. No sooner has Jesus made his announcement that the Kingdom of God has come, than he joins issue with the devil in the demon-possessed man in the synagogue of

Capernaum. This is followed by the cure of Peter's mother-in-law who is sick of a fever. Then the leper is cleansed and restored to society. Then the paralytic is healed and his sins forgiven. Then the man with the withered hand is made whole again. The Kingdom of God is God in effective conflict with evil in all its forms — in conflict with the devil, in conflict with sickness, in conflict with uncleanness, in conflict with sin, in conflict with impotence. The war between light and darkness, good and evil, righteousness and sin, God and the devil, has now come to your very door. Repent, change the direction of your lives, for life's direction is set by this war which God is waging. Repent and believe in the gospel. Commit yourself to participation in this activity of God. This good news of God's action is for you.

How terribly distorted in meaning the words " salvation" and "belief" have become in our day! "Are you saved?" the question is asked, and by it is meant nothing more than an inquiry concerning the condition of our souls. When a war is on, there is only one thing that needs to be safe, and that is the cause for which the war is being fought. If that is safe, all else that needs to be safe will be safe. When there is peace, each person can live pretty much as he likes; but when there is war, the concerns of the individual take second place, if any place at all. There is no time even to go home and say good-by (Luke 9:62). War means that there is introduced into life a new direction, in terms of which the direction of each individual life must swing into position. This is what the New Testament means when it talks about God's righteousness. God's war with evil sets man his life's direction. Henceforth he is called upon to live in alignment with God's "right" — God's *dikē.* So that to be safe means no more and no less than to be a seeker of God's righteousness. He who so seeks finds his salvation added unto him.

Jesus said: "Seek first God's kingdom [not your place in that kingdom] and his righteousness and all these things shall be added unto you. Be not, therefore, anxious for the morrow; for the morrow will be anxious for itself" (Matt. 6:33–34). Tomorrow is God's tomorrow; my hour of decision is today. To live is not to try to make something of myself or for myself; it is to share in God's life, which is life poured out that "whosoever believeth on him" should not die but have eternal life.

One of the great names of our generation is the name of Dietrich Bonhoeffer, who gave his life for Christ in Germany in opposition to Hitler during the war. In his letters and poems written from prison just before his martyrdom he has left a record of the nature of the Christian life that plumbs its very depths. Here is what he says:

"When a man really gives up trying to make something out of himself—a saint, or a converted sinner, or a churchman (a so-called clerical somebody) . . . when in the fullness of tasks, questions, success or ill-hap, experiences and perplexities, a man throws himself into the arms of God . . . then he wakes with Christ in Gethsemane. That is faith, that is *metanoia,* and it is thus that he becomes a man and a Christian" (Dietrich Bonhoeffer, *The Cost of Discipleship,* pp. 19, 20).

"Men go to God when he is sore bestead:
find him poor and scorned, without shelter and bread,
whelmed under weight of the wicked, the weak, the dead.
Christians stand by God in his hour of grieving."

To keep awake with Christ in Gethsemane — what a definition of Christian life that is, and how significant its implications! For it is not easy to keep awake, and even if the soul is willing the flesh is weak. The demand is for constant readiness, for that persistent and consistent discipline of the athlete by which he keeps himself always fit. Christian living cannot be undertaken with *askēsis,* without serious obedience to that admonition of Jesus when he said, " If thy hand cause thee to stumble, cut it off; and if thine eye cause thee to stumble, cast it out " (Mark 9:43, 47).

We who are Christians are too flabby in our interests. We have time for everything for which those who are not dedicated to the cause of Jesus have time. We have money to spare for all the things which others surround their lives with. And we are hoping to seek and serve the Kingdom of God with spare money in spare time. It can't be done. " No soldier gets entangled in civilian pursuits, since his aim is to satisfy the one who enlisted him " (II Tim. 2:4). It is a war in which we are engaged, the war of the great King, and we have to be prepared to live the soldier's life. When you pray, said Jesus, say, " Our Father, give us this day our daily bread." The Greek word translated " daily " means " a soldier's ration." It is food for the soldier for which prayer is being offered, food that he may fight and not that he may live. For man does not live by bread alone. He lives by the word of God. His life is to obey that word. Bread is simply bodily sustenance for the life of obedience.

These lectures are being delivered during Lent, and it is appropriate that the meaning of Lent is underlined

in them. Lent does not mean a period for small acts
of self-denial, when he who loves his pipe goes without
it or he who loves his meat turns vegetarian. This period
of Lent is intended to remind us that we are always in
Lent, that until Jesus comes again in glory the war
is not over and there is no relaxing of the soldier's
discipline. Jesus fasted for forty days in the wilderness,
and during those forty days he seems to have meditated
a great deal on the forty years' journey of his people
from Egypt to Canaan. All his replies to the devil's
temptations are drawn from the record of this period.
We too are in the wilderness on our journey to Canaan,
and Lent is not over till our rest is won.

Indeed, our powerlessness in preaching the gospel
stems from our failure to realize that the Christian
life is lived in Lent. Our lives are too much conformed
to the life of the world; we have become undistinguishable. But, not only have we become undistinguishable;
we have become isolated. We have lost contact with
the world, combatant contact. We would be pressed
by the enemy if we were pressing him; now, however,
we are comfortable in the world. We are behind the
fighting lines. Jesus said that we must be like the city
set upon a hill — distinguishable — and that we must
also be like leaven hid within the lump, not isolated.
Such a life is not easily lived. It is said that one day
G. K. Chesterton, traveling on a train, was absorbed
in reading a book. Suddenly he woke up to his surround-
ings and discovered that he was on a train. But he had
forgotten where he was going. So he got out at the next
station and sent a telegram from there to his wife. The
telegram said, "I am here; where ought I to be?" The

reply came back from her: "Look at your ticket." That
is our predicament as Christians. We have not only
forgotten where we are going; we have even forgotten
that we have a ticket.

There is a wonderful relevance for the Christian in the
words that the prophet Jeremiah addresses to Baruch,
when Baruch breaks out in distress saying, "Woe is
me now! for the Lord hath added sorrow to my pain:
I am weary with my groaning, and I find no rest." To
him, Jeremiah brings God's reply: "Behold, that which
I have built will I break down, and that which I have
planted I will pluck up; and this is the whole land.
And seekest thou great things for thyself? seek them
not; for behold, I will bring evil upon all flesh; but
thy life will I give unto thee for a prey in all places
whither thou goest" (Jer. 45:3-5). God at war, and
life's security shattered by God's action, and God's
servant involved in the war and in the insecurity of
life — that is the dimension in which the Christian life
has to be lived. It is life in the presence of death.

Our first lecture was woven around the theme of
hope, our second around the theme of death, our third
around the theme of love, and this our fourth around
the theme of life. We must now weave all four themes
together, for they belong together in the Christian life.
Hope sets life scanning the far horizons, while death
gives it depth and cleanness of decision. Love lifts it
above the sorrow by which it is surrounded, until it
reaches the source of life itself by its single dedication
to God.

So we come to the end of this series of lectures on
preaching the gospel of the resurrection, and there is

only one thing to say in conclusion. It is to declare the great consummation for which we wait when death itself shall finally be destroyed and sin cast away. We are those on whom the end of the ages has come (I Cor. 10:11). For us the end of death has begun. We live in a world in which death has been conquered. Jesus died and rose again, the first fruits of them that die. And we live already as those to whom belong the promise of the resurrection and the present foretaste of its power. But, when Christ shall have subdued all his enemies, foretaste will give place to the complete reality, and the Kingdom of the Son will become the Kingdom of the Father (I Cor. 15:24). Jesus taught us to pray, " Our Father, thy Kingdom come."

But it is Jesus who is king of our world now. " All authority in heaven and on earth has been given unto me," he said (Matt. 28:18). " God has highly exalted him that at the name of Jesus every knee should bow, and every tongue confess that Jesus Christ is Lord, to the glory of God the Father " (Phil. 2:9–11). " Now we see not yet all things put under man but we see Jesus crowned with glory and honor " (Heb. 2:8, 9). The sign of this Kingdom of Jesus is the cross. He rules from it. It is the rule of relentless love. There is no sheep that is lost that the shepherd is not seeking, no son who is in the far country in search of whom the elder brother will not go. Jesus comes to us as we sit among the pigs, assures us of our Father's welcome, and persuades us to put our hands into his hand as he leads us home.

That is the differentia of the Christian faith — the announcement to us who are in the far country that we are children of God, each one known and loved by

name. And he who makes this announcement is the
risen Christ. It is an announcement made to us now,
not simply an announcement made long ago about which
we read. But what about those who have never heard
this announcement, because no one has introduced them
to the risen Christ? or even those who, having heard
it, have not accepted it? Also, what about those who
lived before Jesus was born? The Christian faith affirms
that Jesus is the judge of all men. This means that all
men will meet him face to face. Is it inconceivable,
then, that there will be those who have not known
him here who will accept him there? He who has learned
to live by the light, however dim the light available to
him may have been, has learned to accept Jesus who
is "the light which lighteth every man" (John 1:9).
It is inconceivable also that there will be those who
have rejected him here, who, when they meet him there,
will accept him; for the Jesus they rejected was a false
Jesus, wrongly presented and wrongly understood?
Indeed, is it inconceivable that even this may happen,
that among those who say here that they have accepted
Jesus, some, when they meet him face to face, will reject
him there? The form of that final meeting we cannot
know, but it will be a form in which acceptance or
rejection of Jesus will both be possible. The Jews who
waited and prayed with great expectation for their
Messiah rejected him when he came. "A man had two
sons; and he went to the first and said, 'Son, go and
work in the vineyard today.' And he answered, 'I will
not'; but afterward he repented and went. And he went
to the second and said the same; and he answered, 'I
go, sir,' but did not go" (Matt. 21:28–30).

But no discussion of man's ultimate destiny can evade a still further question. It is true that there is salvation in no one else but Jesus, for there is no other name under heaven given among men by which we must be saved (Acts 4:12). Man's salvation is bound up with his response to Jesus Christ. But will all men ultimately be saved? Will Jesus succeed in bringing all men home? Or will there always be a hell?

It is a question we cannot escape when we speak about the great consummation when the Father's Kingdom will come. But thank God that, though this is a question we cannot escape asking, it is a question for which we are neither required nor permitted to give an answer. Faith cannot say, "Yes, there will always be a hell"; for hell is never an object of faith. I do not believe in hell; I only know that I can send myself to hell. And where faith cannot answer, "Yes, there will always be a hell," neither is it possible to answer, "No, a time will come when hell will cease to be." Such an answer will be merely a logical deduction from what we know of the love of God, and logic has no standing when we speak of that love. We are simply faced with the fact of hell into which men and women continue to send themselves, and the fact of the cross with which God besieges hell. We are either besiegers with God or besieged.

"Beloved, build up yourselves on your most holy faith and pray in the Holy Spirit, so keeping yourselves within the love of God and waiting for the mercy of our Lord Jesus Christ that ends in life eternal. Snatch some from the fire, and have mercy on the waverers, trembling as you touch them, with loathing for the

garment which the flesh has stained" (Jude 20–23).
That is where we stand, "within the love of God and
waiting for the mercy of our Lord Jesus Christ" (Jude
21).

Let me conclude with a story told by a famous French
bishop to his congregation. (This story was related in
an address by Canon R. E. Davies at Canberra, and is
here repeated from memory.) Three university students
of Paris were walking along the road one Good Friday
afternoon. They noticed crowds of people going to the
churches to make their confession. The students began
to discuss this custom of the "unenlightened," and
talked in rather cynical terms about the survival of
religion which they described as superstition. Suddenly
two of the students turned to the third, who was the
leader among them, and said to him, "Will you go
into this church and tell the priest there what we have
been saying to each other?" "Sure, I will," he said, and
went in. He stood in the queue of those who were
going to their confession, and when his turn came, he
looked at the priest and said, "Father, I have come
here merely to tell you that Christianity is a dying insti-
tution and that religion is a superstition." The priest
looked at the young man keenly and said, "Why did
you come here, my son, to tell me this?" And the
student told him of his conversation with his friends.
The priest listened carefully and then said: "All right,
I want you to do one thing for me before you go. You
accepted the challenge of your friends and came here;
now accept my challenge to you. Walk up to the chancel
and you will find there a large wooden cross and on it
the figure of Jesus crucified. I want you to stand before

that cross and say these words: 'Jesus died for me and I don't care a damn.'" The student looked diffident but, to save face, agreed. He went up and stood before that cross and said it: "Jesus died for me and I don't care a damn." He came back to the priest and said, "I have done it." "Do it once more," said the priest; "after all it means nothing to you." The student went back and looked at the cross for some time and the figure on it, and then he stammered it out: "Jesus died for me and I don't care a damn." He returned to the priest and said, "I have done it; I am going now." The priest stopped him. "Once more," he said, "just once more and you can go." The young man walked up to the chancel and looked at that cross again, and at the Crucified. He stood there for a long time. Then he came back to the priest and said, "Father, can I make my confession now?" The bishop concluded the story with these words: "And, my dear people, that young man was myself."

The signature of life is written in blood.

"Now unto him that is able to guard you from stumbling, and to set you before the presence of his glory without blemish in exceeding joy, to the only God our Saviour, through Jesus Christ our Lord, be glory, majesty, dominion and power, before all time, and now, and for evermore. Amen."